D0174933

The Little Book
of
HAND
SHADOWS

Created and Drawn by
PHILA H. WEBB

Verses by
JANE CORBY

RUNNING PRESS
PHILADELPHIA · LONDON

Library of Congress Cataloging-in-Publication Number
90-52549
ISBN 0-89471-852-5
This book may be ordered by mail from the publisher.
Please add $1.00 for postage and handling for each copy.
But try your bookstore first!
Running Press Book Publishers
125 South Twenty-second Street
Philadelphia, Pennsylvania 19103-4399

Table of Contents

The First Moving Pictures

Shadow pictures were really the first motion pictures. Boys and girls have been enjoying them for—oh, years and years!—ever since the first grandmother discovered that the shadow of her hand on the wall looked like a swan's head; or perhaps some child first made the great discovery. At any rate it was long ago. Since then, people have been thinking of new ways of holding their fingers to get different shadows, so that now there is a long list of animals and objects that can be brought to life in shadow pictures.

The great advantage of the shadow kind of "movies" lies in the fact that nothing is needed except a light and a flat, light-colored surface; these are to be found in every home. The stronger the light and the whiter the flat surface, the clearer the shadow picture will be. A sheet tacked against

the wall or thrown over a door makes the finest screen in the world, and the ordinary electric bulb makes the right kind of light. If the rest of the room can be darkened as much as possible, the shadow picture on the screen will show up much clearer by contrast.

Pictures of different sizes are obtained by holding the hands nearer the light, or farther from it. A little practice is required in some of the more difficult poses, but there is nothing hard about any of them. Probably, in trying to get these pictures, you'll accidentally invent

new poses of your own. That's part of the fun of shadow pictures—no one ever quite knows what is going to appear on the screen!

—Jane Corby

A SNAIL

Here is a snail, with his house on his back,

No wonder he's slow — with so heavy a pack!

But then, he is not in a hurry, I s'pose,

For he is at home, wherever he goes!

Suggestions: Move both hands, very slowly, forward and the snail will appear to be on his way. Move your whole left hand a little, from side to side, to make the house sway as he goes.

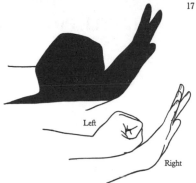

Left

Right

Every once in a while stop and bend the fingers of your right hand forward and backward, as if Mr. Snail were tossing his little horns.

A LITTLE PIG

This little pig went to market and bought

All the things he was sent for, as little pigs
     ought.

And he didn't cry "Wee!" but like a good pig,

He hurried home happily, jig-a-jig-jig!

Suggestions: The little pig's curly tail will curl
and uncurl very nicely if you curl and uncurl
the little finger of your left hand. Making him

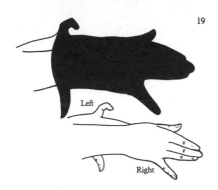

jig is harder, but you can do it if you can move the little finger of your right hand and the thumb of your left at the same time.

A PANTHER

Here's a panther, fearful beast!

Cannot pet him in the least.

Panthers live in woods, and oh!

We are glad to have it so.

Suggestions: As the panther is such an exceedingly fierce creature, it is best to have him on the screen as short a time as possible.

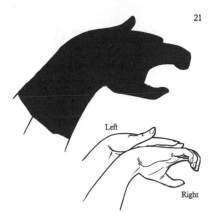

Open and shut his jaws a few times and let him vanish.

DAPPLE GRAY

Here is the pony, whose name is Dapple Gray,

Once borrowed by a lady to ride a mile away;

She whipped him and she lashed him – oh,
how could she do that?

He's such a knowing pony he only needs a pat.

Suggestions: You can make Dapple Gray go
anywhere you like, forward or backward, by
moving your hands along the screen. Raise and

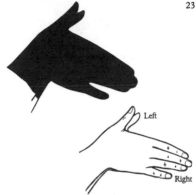

Left

Right

lower your two hands, held in position, as you move them along, and Dapple Gray will appear to be galloping.

A DOG

Now here's a pet for girls and boys;

He has a bark that makes a noise!

He plays with children when it's light,

And keeps the thieves away at night.

Suggestions: Lower and raise first one thumb, then the other, as if the dog were pricking up his ears. You can also open and shut his

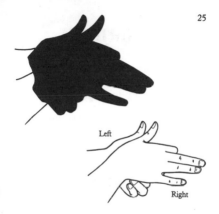

Left

Right

mouth, and if you bark at the same time, it will make the shadow picture more lifelike.

A TORTOISE

This is the tortoise who once won a race,

By going at no very furious pace;

He beat a swift rabbit, but only because

He kept going always, without any pause.

Suggestions: Perseverance, you see, always wins. Keep trying and you'll make as good-looking a tortoise as you see on this page. Move

the two first fingers of your left hand, very slowly, from side to side, the way a tortoise moves.

POLLY WANTS A CRACKER!

Here is the Polly of whom you've heard tell,

She wants a nice cracker – you know the words well.

Nice Polly – so pretty! A cracker she'll get,

Though we haven't got one to give to her yet.

Suggestions: Warn your audience to keep away from Polly's dangerous-looking beak. You can show how she would eat a cracker, if she had one, by bringing the three fingers of your left

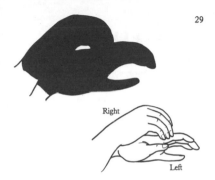

hand down upon the little finger, letting the
upper beak protrude a little, as a polly's does.
An assistant can put a cracker in Polly's mouth,
if you like.

AN ELEPHANT

Here's an elephant, you can tell by his lengthy
nose,
Comes of poking it in others' business, I
suppose.
Let the elephant's long nose be a lesson to
you—
Keep your nose at home or you may grow
nosy-looking too!

Suggestions: Have someone offer the elephant
peanuts. With practice you will be able to carry

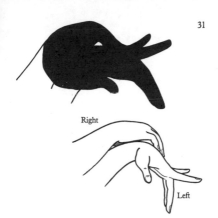

Right

Left

a peanut with the two middle fingers of your left hand, which form the trunk, to the mouth.

A BILLY-GOAT

Here's old Billy Goat, with a beard on his
    chin;

You can't keep him out for he'll butt his way in.

He will butt his way through a fence or a door,

Eat all that's in sight and go hunting for more.

Suggestions: Billy Goat is not expected to do
more than waggle his beard. The thumb of

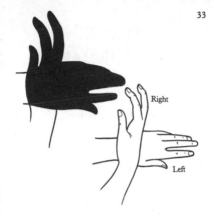

your left hand, which forms the beard, can
waggle easily in this position.

TURKEY IN THE HAY

This is turkey in the hay,

Who gobbles all the livelong day;

You cannot catch him if you try,

For he can run and he can fly.

Suggestions: When you have made the turkey gobble, by moving the forefinger of your left hand up and down against the little finger of your right hand, you ought to move the three

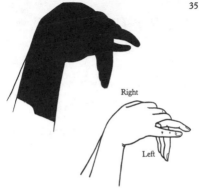

fingers of the left hand that form the turkey's wattles, because when a turkey gobbles his wattles shake.

GOOSEY, GOOSEY, GANDER

This is old Goosey, who wandered about,

Upstairs and downstairs, indoors and out;

Goosey, Goosey, Gander likes to strut around

To see if any stray corn is lying on the ground.

Suggestions: Open and shut Goosey's beak by
moving your fingers, and every now and then
dip your hands, held together, downward

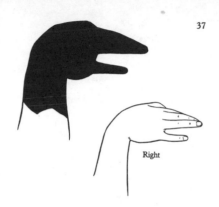

Right

sharply, as if Goosey had stopped for a kernel of corn.

A MOOSE

This is a moose, who roams the wild wood;

He does not care for cities – indeed no moose
    could.

A moose in a city must live in a zoo;

I am glad that I've made a wild moose, aren't
    you?

Suggestions: Moose are in the habit of tossing
their heads from time to time. Toss your hands,

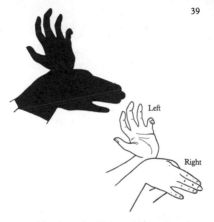

Left

Right

up and backward a little, without changing
their position, to get a moose-like effect.

A WOODPECKER

This smart little bird is a doctor of trees;

Our woods would soon die without doctors
    like these.

Peck! Peck! Not a bug can escape her keen sight;

Now you watch as sharply and get this bird right.

Suggestions: Move your hands forward
quickly, and back again, as if the woodpecker
were darting at an insect. The forefinger of
your left hand, extended, gives the perch. The

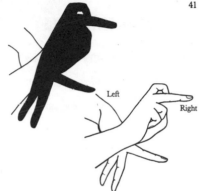

thumb of your left hand, clasping the little finger of the same hand, keeps both out of sight.

OLD KING COLE

Here is Old King Cole – the merry old soul!

He wears his crown on the top of his head,

Perhaps he is waiting for his pipe and bowl.

And is always merry, as I have said.

Suggestions: Old King Cole is pretty easy to make. If you have a pipe handy, you can let him hold it in his mouth – letting the little

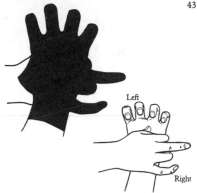

finger of your right hand keep it in place against the wrist of your left hand.

THE COURT JESTER

This jester looks quite solemn, but clowns are
    apt to be;
Their business is to make us laugh, not laugh
    themselves, you see.
It's funny just to see him, but when he shows
    his tricks,
And wig-wags with his long nose, you'll laugh
    enough for six.

Suggestions: The third finger of your left
hand, which forms the jester's nose, can be
wriggled to make him look funnier. You can

Right

Left

make his cap bob, too, by moving your whole
right hand without moving your fingers.

AN ALLIGATOR

This is a 'gator; how well he must bite

With all those long teeth that are out in plain sight!

I hope that no 'gator comes snapping 'round me,

For they are quite dangerous as I can see.

Suggestions: Move your two hands, without disturbing your fingers, together and apart again quickly, so that the alligator's jaws will

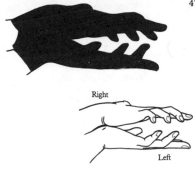

Right

Left

snap. At the same time move forward along the screen, as if the creature were traveling at a rapid rate.

A COCKATOO

Here's a very fine bird – the gay cockatoo!

A lot of good tricks this birdie can do.

He can bow when you tell him and wave his
     fine crest;

Oh, he is an actor that ranks with the best!

Suggestions: Bend both hands forward to make
the cockatoo bow, and wave the fingers of your
left hand to make him wave his crest. The

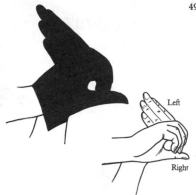

Left

Right

thumb of your right hand, when bent upward and straightened quickly, makes the bird appear to be eating.

A RABBIT

See this plump, pretty little rabbit,

She has a most engaging habit

Of wriggling both her lengthy ears,

Whenever some strange sound she hears!

Suggestions: The last three fingers on your left hand, that form the ears, can be easily wriggled, in imitation of a bunny. The rabbit can

also be made to scratch her nose. Use the right forefinger, which forms one of her paws, for this trick.

THE CROWING COCK

This is the cock that crowed in the morn

Because he wanted a breakfast of corn;

He woke the farmer, bent with age—

You'll find him on another page.

Suggestions: This looks a great deal harder than it is, but if you get your left hand into position first you will see that it is easy to

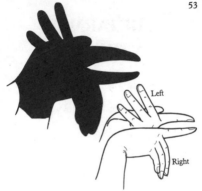

manage the right one. Show how the cock crows by opening and shutting the two forefingers that form the beak.

THE FARMER
IN THE DELL

Here is the Farmer in the Dell

Who took a wife – you know him well.

Heigh-ho! The farmers only know

How oats and beans and barley grow.

Suggestions: Notice that the farmer's nose is
the forefinger of the left hand caught between
the little finger and the third finger of the right

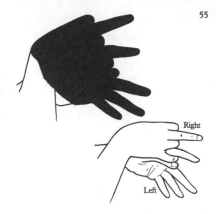

hand. His whiskers will wag if you move the
last three fingers of your left hand.

A CRAB

This crab is alive for she's never been caught,

She runs from all danger as every crab ought.

She has many fine legs and they help her run
fast;

Just watch and you'll see her go scurrying past.

Suggestions: Move all the fingers on both
hands as you move your hands forward along

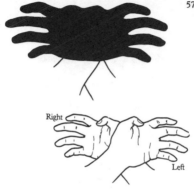

the screen. Remember that a crab goes a little sideways, not straight ahead.

A FROG

This is the frog who would, you know,

Across the field a-wooing go.

He went to woo Miss Mouse, they tell,

Of this frog who lived in a well.

Suggestions: Move your whole right hand, gently, and you will see the frog's throat throbbing in a lifelike manner.

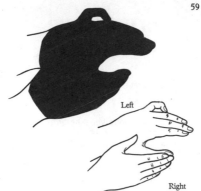

Left

Right

OLD MOTHER HUBBARD

Here's the old woman whose troubles were
    many,

Who looked for a bone when she didn't have any.

No matter; she made shadow pictures instead

For her dog—he forgot that he hadn't been fed!

Suggestions: By moving the two middle fingers
of your left hand, after you have them in position, you can make Mother Hubbard appear

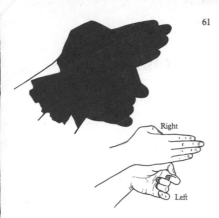

Right

Left

to be talking. Or by moving your little finger a tiny bit, you can make her chin wobble in a funny way.

MOTHER HUBBARD'S DOG

This is her dog; he is begging, you see,

For more shadow pictures – how clever is he!

He can wriggle his ears to express his delight,

And wag his tail, too, if you're making him right.

Suggestions: This delighted dog, who appears to be smiling, can be made to look as if he were barking, if you move the two middle fingers of your right hand, keeping them together, and

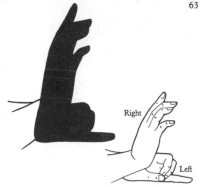

move your little finger at the same time. Wag
his tail by wagging the thumb of your left
hand, and wriggle his ears by wriggling the
forefinger of your right hand.

A KANGAROO

This is, you see, a kangaroo;

What jumping stunts this beast can do!

In fact, she never has to run;

She jumps instead, and thinks it fun.

Suggestions: Tip your right hand forward and backward rapidly as you move both hands

Right

Left

across the screen. The kangaroo will appear to be jumping.

TWO FLYING BIRDS

Here are two birds, see how they fly!

Away they go, up to the sky.

They're blackbirds, maybe, or else crows;

They fly so fast that no one knows!

Suggestions: Move the two hands across the
screen, one following the other. Then let them

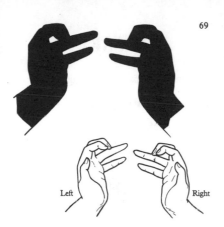

Left   Right

your fingers. Let your hands sway as if the
birds were being rocked in their nest.

A SNAKE

This dreadful snake as black as night,

Is all prepared, I think to bite.

A snake will always lift his head

When he is angry, it is said.

Suggestions: Cut two very narrow strips of paper for fangs, and hold them between your first and second fingers.

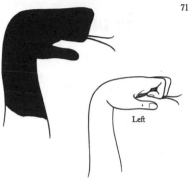

Left

A HIPPOPOTAMUS

The hippo likes to take his ease

In squashy mud up to his knees.

One simply can't grow fond of him —

He has so little life and vim!

Suggestions: Move the two jaws together, very slowly, which is the way a hippopotamus does most things.

Right

Left

A SLY WEASEL

Here's a sly weasel, watch her creep

And suddenly she'll give a leap.

She hunts by night and sleeps by day

And sleepy chickens are her prey!

Suggestions: Move your hands, together, slowly across the screen, then tip them suddenly

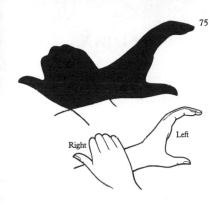

forward, as if the weasel had pounced upon some unsuspecting creature.

A CLOWN

This is the clown who ends the book;

He has a very merry look.

He's quite as good as all the rest,

And hopes, I think, you'll vote him best!

Suggestions: You can give the clown a dreadfully long nose by stretching out the middle finger of your left hand, after you have it in

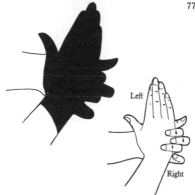

Left

Right

position. Make the clown talk by wriggling upward the little finger on your left hand and say "Good-night" for him.

This book has been bound using handcraft methods, and Smyth-sewn to ensure durability.

The dust jacket was designed by Toby Schmidt.

The interior was designed by Judith Barbour Osborne.

The text was typeset in Plantin with Fenice Bold by Commcor Communications Corporation, Philadelphia, Pennsylvania.

This book was adapted from *Shadowgraphs Anyone Can Make*, first published in 1927 by Stoll & Edwards Co., New York.